FIDDLE TUNES FOR FLATPICKERS GUITAR

BY BOB GRANT

T0078778

PLAYBACK+

Speed • Pitch • Balance • Loop

To access companion recorded performances and
accompaniments online, visit:
www.halleonard.com/mylibrary

6546-3756-0947-5734

ISBN 978-0-8256-8752-5
Order No. OK65142

HAL•LEONARD®

Visit Hal Leonard Online at
www.halleonard.com

Contact us:
Hal Leonard
7777 West Bluemound Road
Milwaukee, WI 53213
Email: info@halleonard.com

In Europe, contact:
Hal Leonard Europe Limited
42 Wigmore Street
Marylebone, London, W1U 2RN
Email: info@halleonardeurope.com

In Australia, contact:
Hal Leonard Australia Pty. Ltd.
4 Lentara Court
Cheltenham, Victoria, 3192 Australia
Email: info@halleonard.com.au

Acknowledgments
Thanks to my many students, who have inspired me to pick apart
what I do unconsciously and demand that I explain it clearly—it
has made me a better player and a special thank you to
Tonya Upchurch for putting up with me.

Steven Berryessa, for whom most of these transcriptions where written out for.

All interior photography by Herb Wise
Project editor: Felipe Orozco
Interior design and layout: Len Vogler
Cover design: Stacy Boge

TABLE OF CONTENTS

PREFACE 4

ONLINE AUDIO TRACK LIST 4

INTRODUCTION 5

HOW TO USE THIS BOOK 6

TABLATURE 7

READING MUSIC 8

PICKING TECHNIQUE 9

THE TUNES—KEY OF A 10

    OLD JOE CLARK 10

    SALT CREEK 11

    SALLY GOODIN' 12

    BILL CHEATHAM 13

    CHEROKEE SHUFFLE 14

    FIRE ON THE MOUNTAIN 15

    SWEET LIZA JANE 16

    DEVIL'S DREAM 17

    RED HAIRED BOY 18

    BIG MON 19

    CATTLE IN THE CANE 20

    CLUCK OLD HEN 21

THE TUNES—KEY OF C 22

    TEXAS GALES 22

    BILLY IN THE LOW GROUND 24

    BOSTON BOY 25

THE TUNES—KEY OF D 26

    WHISKEY BEFORE BREAKFAST 26

    SOLDIER'S JOY 27

    LIBERTY 28

    EIGHTH OF JANUARY 29

    FISHER'S HORNPIPE 30

    ARKANSAS TRAVELER 31

    SAILOR'S HORNPIPE 32

    TEMPERANCE REEL 33

    BLACKBERRY BLOSSOM 34

    TURKEY IN THE STRAW 36

CONCLUSION 37

LISTENING SUGGESTIONS 38

PREFACE

The history of flatpicking fiddle tunes on guitar is relatively brief. Although the guitar has held a very important place in all kinds of music, especially country and bluegrass, its role had always been rhythmic. The guitar had always supported rather than led soloists on instruments such as the fiddle, mandolin, and banjo.

It wasn't until the early 1960s that guitarists decided that they too could step out front and play the hot fiddle tunes. The first guitar player to do it convincingly was a North Carolinian named Arthel "Doc" Watson.

Doc inspired many guitarists, including Clarence White, to come up with highly developed and personal styles, but it wasn't until Dan Crary released his *Bluegrass Guitar* record in the early 1970s that the instrument was elevated to the same status as the fiddle, mandolin, and banjo on the contest circuit.

Nowadays it is no longer a surprise to hear a guitar player step up and take a solo on a fiddle tune with a bluegrass band—in fact, it's almost expected.

ONLINE AUDIO TRACK LIST

1. Old Joe Clark
2. Salt Creek
3. Sally Goodin'
4. Bill Cheatham
5. Cherokee Shuffle
6. Fire on the Mountain
7. Sweet Liza Jane
8. Devil's Dream
9. Red Haired Boy
10. Big Mon
11. Cattle in the Cane
12. Cluck Old Hen
13. Texas Gales
14. Billy in the Low Ground
15. Boston Boy
16. Whiskey Before Breakfast
17. Soldier's Joy
18. Liberty
19. Eighth of January
20. Fisher's Hornpipe
21. Arkansas Traveler
22. Sailor's Hornpipe
23. Temperance Reel
24. Blackberry Blossom
25. Turkey in the Straw

INTRODUCTION

This book was designed to help guitar players who are interested in flatpicking build a repertoire of commonly played fiddle tunes, as well as provide examples of the most commonly used techniques.

Since most of these traditional tunes have been passed around from musician to musician (in some cases over hundreds of years) and have gradually been changed by the musicians who play them, the versions presented here are interpretations rather than exact melodies.

While the melody of the tunes is emphasized in these arrangements, they will frequently include variations on the theme, interesting ornamentations, or alternate parts.

As you learn these tunes, you will recognize and learn different techniques used in certain situations such as slides, double stops, fiddle shuffles, tremolos, double-time ornaments, and syncopations. Once you learn these techniques, you will be able to apply them to other songs.

Arthel "Doc" Watson

HOW TO USE THIS BOOK

Each tune in this book presents a new challenge. To help you, a brief explanation of the challenging passages, fingerings, positions, or trouble spots preceding every song.

The accompanying online audio has a demonstration track for each example that allows you to hear the guitar alone or the accompaniment without the guitar by just panning the balance control all the way left (accompaniment) or right (guitar).

After learning the tunes, get them up to speed so that you can practice along with the audio tracks—this will prepare you for playing with a group.

Every tune is presented in standard notation and *tablature*, which eliminates any ambiguities that might go into what fingering might be best for a specific passage or phrase.

Tablature (TAB) is music notation shorthand for stringed instruments and is very easy to read. The six horizontal lines represent the six strings of the guitar, from high to low. The number indicates the fret and the line tells you which string to press down. It's similar to reading chord diagrams, but sideways.

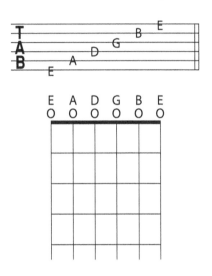

Common TAB Symbols

Hammer-On
Pick the indicated string, then sound an upper note by hammering on to the string with the finger.

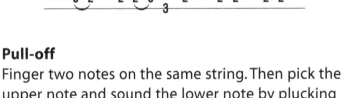

Pull-off
Finger two notes on the same string. Then pick the upper note and sound the lower note by plucking the string with the fretting finger.

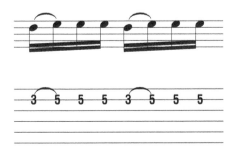

Slide
Play the first note normally, then slide the left-hand finger to the second note. A slide line connects the notes of a slide. When a slide line comes from no other note (as in many cases in the following arrangements), slide up or down from a point a few frets above or below the note.

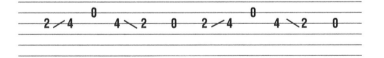

READING MUSIC

The next thing you need to be able to do is to apply rhythm to the numbers on the TAB lines. To achieve this, you will have to look at the standard notation staff above the TAB.

At the beginning of the song you will see the *time signature*. The top number tells you how many beats are in a measure and the bottom number tells you what note gets the beat:

There are five rhythmic values that you are going to need to know: whole notes, half notes, quarter notes, eighth notes, and sixteenth notes.

If the time signature is ⁴⁄₄ it means that a *quarter note* gets *one* beat. Therefore, a *whole note* will get *four* beats, and a *half note* will last *two* beats. Each quarter note can also be divided into *two eighth notes*, or *four sixteenth notes.*

whole note

half notes

quarter notes

eighth notes

sixteenth notes

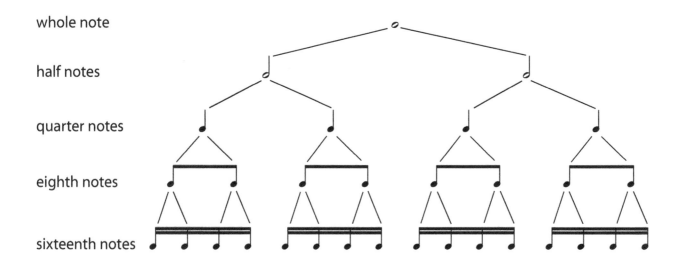

A note's rhythm is identified by the flag attached to its stem:

eighth notes

sixteenth notes

Consecutive eighth or sixteenth notes can be *beamed* together:

beamed eighth notes

beamed sixteenth notes

Proper picking technique is essential when playing fiddle tunes. You have to move your pick in the right direction to achieve the right sense of power and dynamics that each song requires. The following patterns will help you achieve the proper picking technique.

Down-Up Pattern

Let's take a look at a group of four sixteenth notes (one beat). The first and third notes are strong beats (also called *downbeats*) and would be picked with *downstrokes,* represented by ⊓ (down); the second and fourth notes are weak beats (also called *upbeats*) and would be picked with *upstrokes,* represented by ∨ (up). This creates a consistent *down-up-down-up* (DUDU) pattern.

Down-Down-Up Pattern

In the following example, the pick directions stay the same. You are just removing the second note of the pattern but keeping the pick direction intact. This is a *down-down-up* pattern (DDU).

Down-Up-Down Pattern

Remove the fourth note and you will get a *down-up-down* pattern (DUD).

Down-Up-Up Pattern

Remove the third note and you have a *down-up-up* pattern (DUU). This pattern never changes—no exceptions—it creates a strict alternate picking style that provides the power and volume that you'll need for playing an acoustic guitar. If you break this pattern everything that comes after will sound rough and clumsy.

THE TUNES—KEY OF A

Old Joe Clark contains the *double-stop fiddle shuffle* technique. The fiddle shuffle occurs on the third and fourth beats of the second measure.

The fiddle shuffle always starts with a DDU picking pattern followed by strict DUDU picking pattern.

This technique is featured in many of the tunes; practice it slowly to develop speed and accuracy.

OLD JOE CLARK

This tune is also known as "Salt River," and is one of the most played fiddle tunes. Watch out for measure 4 of the [A] section, as it has a position shift that can be tricky.

The first measure of the [B] section has a pretty big stretch. A good way to approach it is by using the first finger on the G, the middle finger on the A, and the pinky on the B followed by another position shift.

SALT CREEK

Track 2

Key of A
Capo 2nd Fret

Traditional

THE TUNES—KEY OF A

The arrangement of this tune is one of the most straightforward reading notations available. The challenging part of this song is the syncopation in the second and fourth measures of the B section.

This B section breaks up the sixteenth-note momentum of the rest of the tune. Be careful to give these notes their proper duration or you will throw the rest of the tune off.

SALLY GOODIN'

Traditional

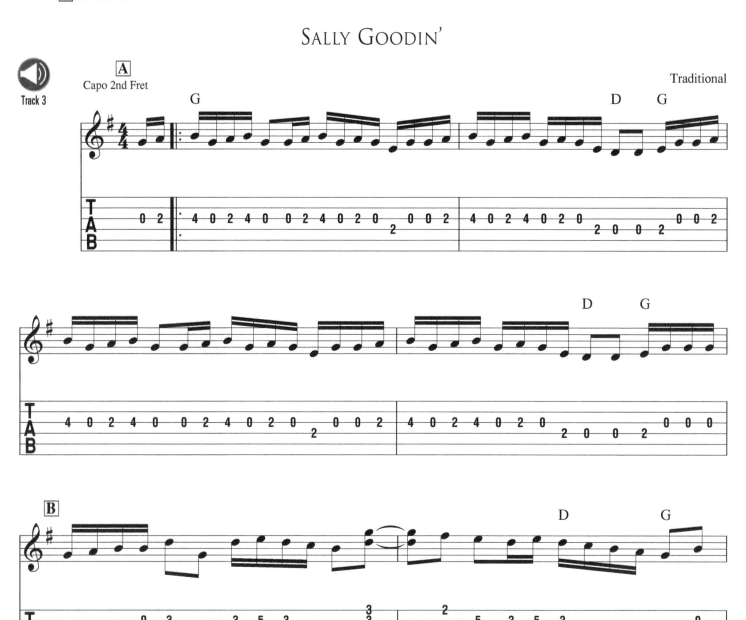

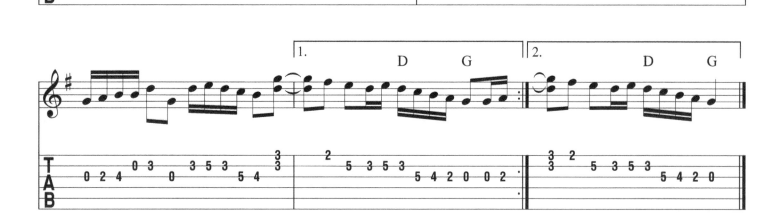

Check out the G natural in the second measure, it gives this tune a bluesy sound. The [B] section is made up of lots of arpeggios.

There is a pretty crazy stretch to get to the A in the first and second measures. Remember to use strict alternate picking and practice very slowly, especially the [B] section.

BILL CHEATHAM

Track 4

Capo 2nd Fret

Traditional

THE TUNES—KEY OF A

Be sure to use the correct fingering in the B section.

Notice the pull-off on the second beat of measures 1, 2, and 3.

CHEROKEE SHUFFLE

Track 5

Capo 2nd Fret

Traditional

This song is usually played really fast, so there is no time for any fancy stuff—just play it. There are only a few places where you are not playing sixteenth notes; therefore, the picking feels similar to an unbroken sentence.

Be sure to use the DUU picking on the third beat of the first and third measure—if you break the picking pattern, everything after it will fall apart.

FIRE ON THE MOUNTAIN

Track 6

Capo 2nd Fret

Traditional

THE TUNES—KEY OF A

This song has a lot of fiddle shuffles. Be sure to play them cleanly because they go by pretty fast and can sound sloppy if you are not careful. Practice this tune very slowly at first; you'll develop speed gradually.

Eventually you will be able to play fiddle shuffles at almost any speed.

Watch out for the pull-offs in the A section and the forward and reverse slides in the B section.

SWEET LIZA JANE

This tune gives the impression that there are two fiddles playing. The key to this song is not playing it too fast—take it easy.

Use alternate picking in the B section. You have to jump a string in measures 1 and 3 to get the double fiddle sound. Skipping a string will seem weird at first, but a little practice goes a long way.

DEVIL'S DREAM

Track 8

Traditional

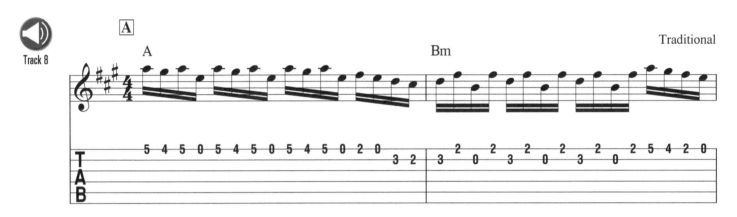

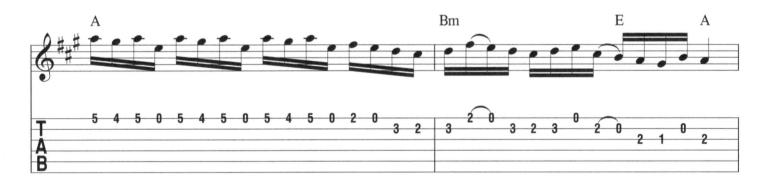

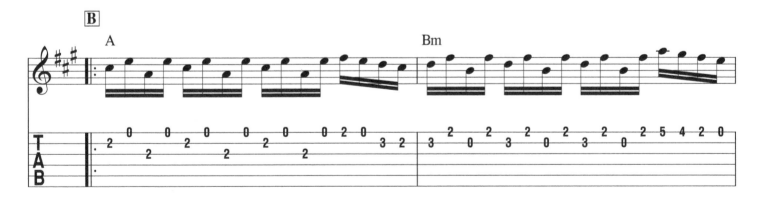

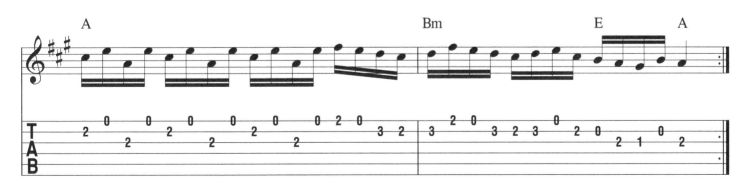

THE TUNES—KEY OF A

This tune has a couple of trouble spots in both left and right hands. The first two beats of the first measure have a tricky grouping of sixteenth notes; pay attention to the pick markings.

Watch out for the pinky stretch in the first and second endings of both the A and B sections.

RED HAIRED BOY

Traditional

This is a classic Bill Monroe tune—a real barnburner. Practice this song slowly and build up speed gradually. Use your first finger to play the first A and C of the second measure.

BIG MON

Track 10

Capo 2nd Fret

Bill Monroe

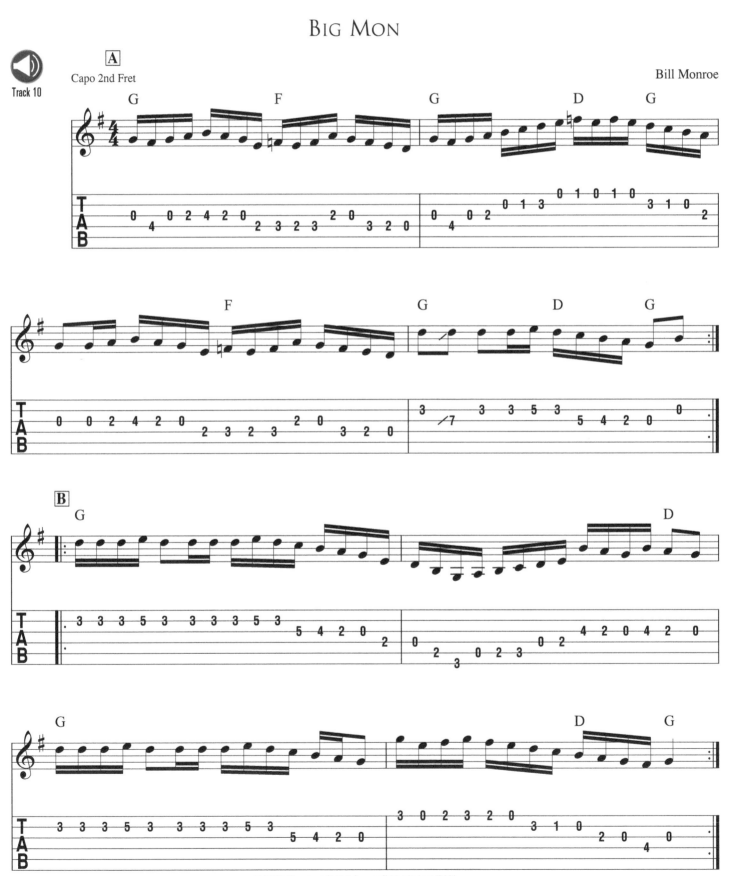

THE TUNES—KEY OF A

This tune is fairly straightforward as far as playing goes, just look out for a couple of slides to the unison. Use your first finger to play the low G in the B section.

There is a really cool change from A major to A minor going from the A part to the B part.

CATTLE IN THE CANE

Traditional

Track 11

Capo 2nd Fret

This is an old-fashioned arrangement of this classic tune. The feel is the most important aspect when playing this song.

Watch out for the double stops in the B part.

CLUCK OLD HEN

Track 12

Capo 2nd Fret

Traditional

THE TUNES—KEY OF C

The following three tunes share common parts. The **B** part of "Texas Gales" is also the **B** part of "Billy in the Low Ground," and its **C** part is the **B** part of "Boston Boy." When you learn "Texas Gales" you will also have learned the B part to both of the other tunes.

Watch out for a tricky spot on the fourth beat of the second measure of "Boston Boy." Listen to the recording to get the phrasing right.

TEXAS GALES

Traditional

Track 13

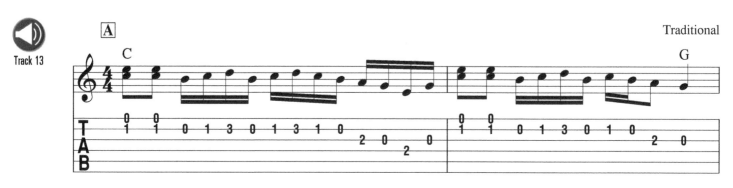

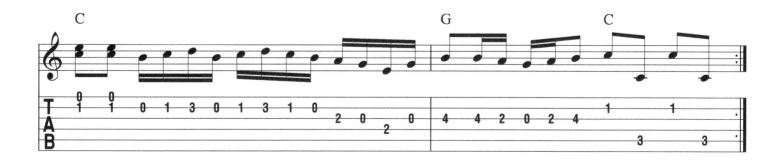

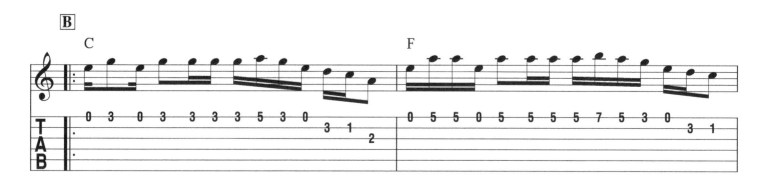

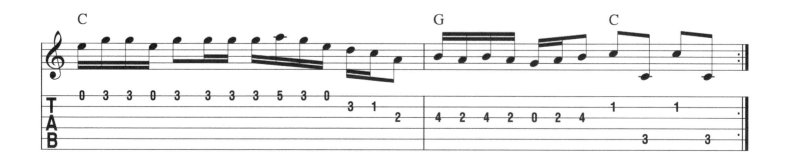

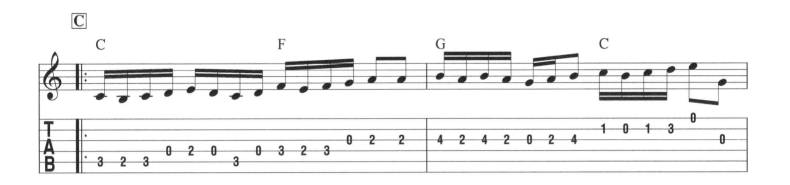

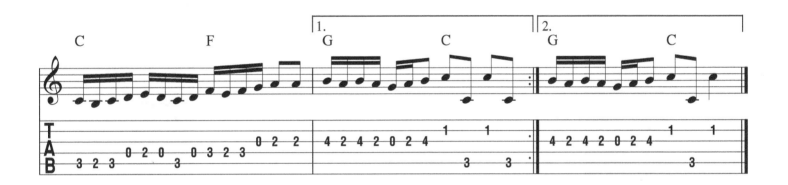

Billy in the Low Ground

Track 14

Traditional

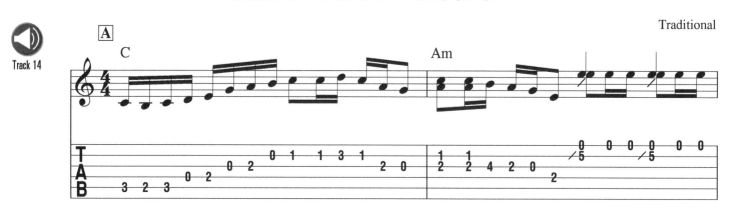

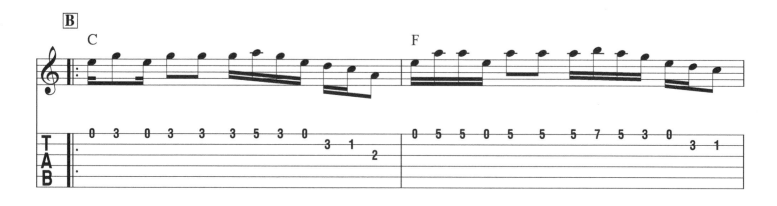

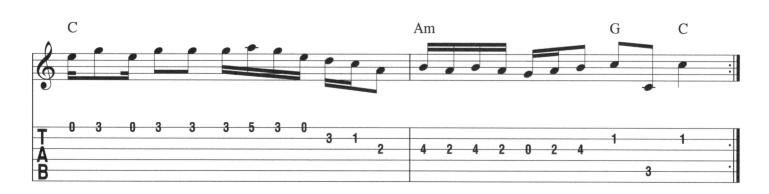

Boston Boy

Traditional

THE TUNES—KEY OF D

The melody and the chords work great in this bluegrass favorite. There is an arpeggio on the first beat of the B section where you have to pick across three strings very quickly; practice this passage until you can play it at speed.

Another challenging passage on the B section is the last beat of the second measure. You have to bar the A and the Cs on the G and B strings with your index finger to be able to play this passage smoothly at speed.

WHISKEY BEFORE BREAKFAST

Traditional

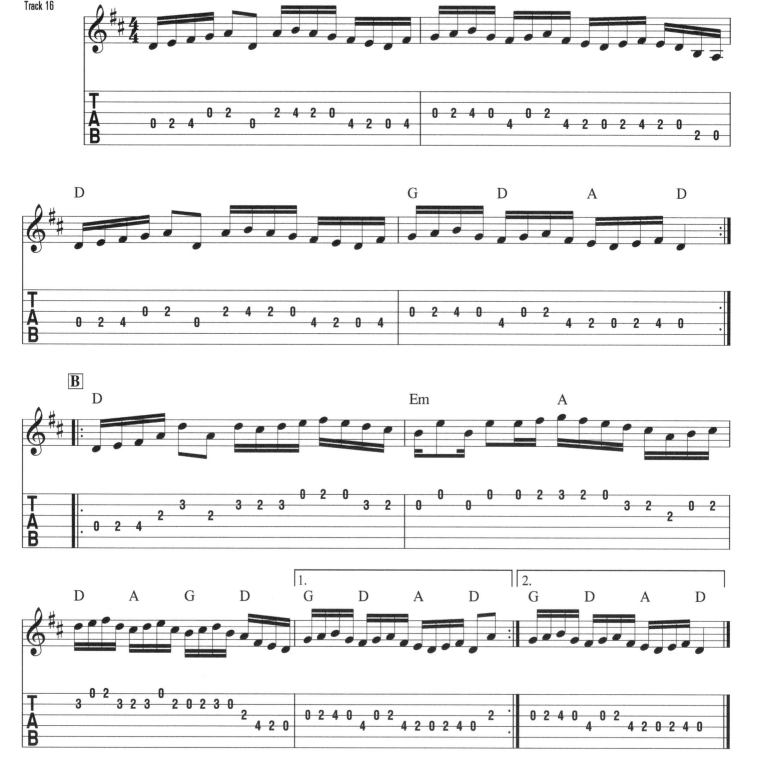

Most people find the quick up and down slide in the B section to be the most difficult part of the tune.

Again, have patience and practice it slowly, gradually working it up to speed. Listen to the recording to get the correct phrasing.

SOLDIER'S JOY

Traditional

Track 17

THE TUNES—KEY OF D

Ben Franklin is said to have wanted this tune to be our national anthem—or so goes the story. Make sure you play it as smooth as possible. The A section starts with a three-string bar at the second fret.

In the B section, the third beat of the first measure is an arpeggio across four strings; it should be played with alternate-pick strokes just as any other sixteenth-note grouping. This is the trickiest part of the tune—once you've mastered it, you're home free.

LIBERTY

Track 18

You may recognize this tune from Johnny Horton's 1960s hit "The Battle of New Orleans."

Be careful with the fourth measure of the A section, it seems clumsy at first but with practice it will become second nature.

EIGHTH OF JANUARY

Track 19

Traditional

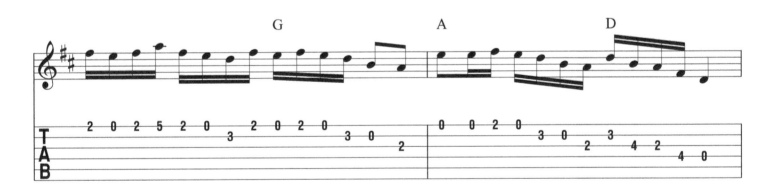

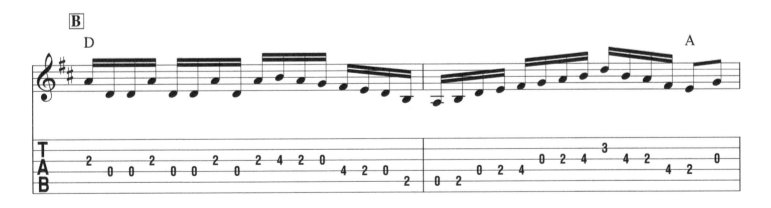

THE TUNES—KEY OF D

Start this tune with an upstroke and everything else will fall nicely into place. Keep your index and ring finger down on the C notes in the [A] section, it will help you get a smooth legato sound.

Listen to the recording to hear an example of this.

FISHER'S HORNPIPE

This is one of the great traditional American melodies, right up there with "Amazing Grace" and "Home Sweet Home."

Play the double stops at the beginning as if you were playing a fiddle, this will give it a classic old-time sound. Be sure to let the open string ring freely to get the right sound.

ARKANSAS TRAVELER

Track 21

Traditional

THE TUNES—KEY OF D

Commonly known as the "Popeye theme," no book of fiddle tunes would be complete without this old gem. This song has an interesting mix of leaps, rhythmic variations, and arpeggios.

SAILOR'S HORNPIPE

Traditional

The first and fourth measures are the most challenging spots in this tune. By now, you know the drill: practice slowly and increase speed once you know the material.

The fourth measure of the [B] section is a little weird but sounds very interesting. Listen to the recording.

TEMPERANCE REEL

Traditional

Track 23

THE TUNES—KEY OF G

This song is one of the most-played fiddle tunes—it's important that you know this one.

As always, watch the pick direction, especially in the B section.

BLACKBERRY BLOSSOM

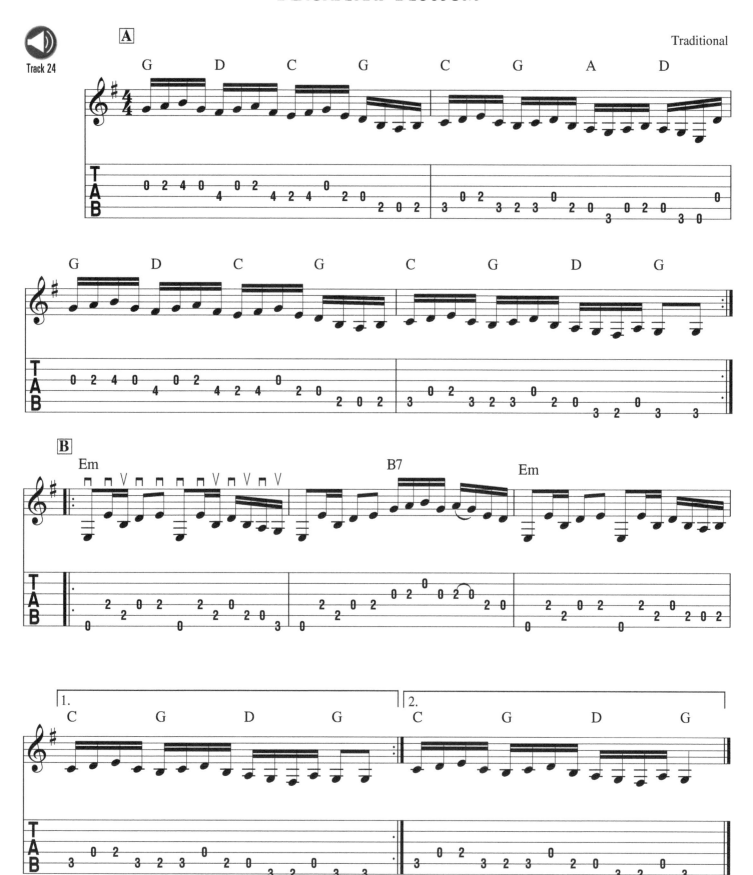

Track 24

Traditional

BLACKBERRY BLOSSOM
ALTERNATIVE A SECTION

THE TUNES—KEY OF G

The first measure of this song feels like it's being played backwards. Practice that part slowly for a while before moving on.

The double stops in section B can be tricky; isolate them and practice slowly until you can get them to sound clean.

TURKEY IN THE STRAW

Traditional

CONCLUSION

This collection of tunes should serve as a good starting point for guitarists who are trying to build a solid repertoire, or as a reference for someone looking for new approaches and techniques for songs they already know. There is a balance between the basic arrangements of the tunes and interesting embellishments that would help guitarists of all levels. I hope that you enjoy playing these tunes as much as I have over the years. Good luck!

LISTENING SUGGESTIONS

Old-Time

Johnson, Earl. *Complete Recorded Works Vol.1 1927*
(Document 8005)

Kessinger, Clark. *Old-Time Music with Fiddle & Guitar*
(Rounder 0004)

McMichen, Clayton. *The Traditional Years*
(Davis Unlimited 33032)

Robertson, Eck. *Old-Time Texas Fiddler 1922-1929*
(County 3515)

Stokes, Lowe. *Lowe Stokes Vol.1 1927-1930*
(Document 8045)

Bluegrass

Baker, Kenny. *Frost on the Pumpkin*
(County 2731)

Monroe, Bill. *Country Music Hall of Fame*
(MCA 10082)

Presenting the Best in
BLUEGRASS

THE REAL BLUEGRASS BOOK

This new collection gathers over 150 bluegrass favorites presented in the world-famous Real Book format. Songs include: Ballad of Jed Clampett • Bill Cheatham • Down to the River to Pray • Foggy Mountain Top • I'm Goin' Back to Old Kentucky • John Henry • Old Train • Pretty Polly • Rocky Top • Sally Goodin • Wildwood Flower • and more.

00310910 C Instruments......................... $35.00

BLUEGRASS

Guitar Play-Along

The Guitar Play-Along Series will help you play your favorite songs quickly and easily! Just follow the tab, listen to the CD to hear how the guitar should sound, and then play along using the separate backing tracks. 8 songs: Duelin' Banjos • Foggy Mountain Breakdown • Gold Rush • I Am a Man of Constant Sorrow • Nine Pound Hammer • Orange Blossom Special • Rocky Top • Wildwood Flower.

00699910 Book/CD Pack...................... $15.99

BLUEGRASS GUITAR CLASSICS

Includes standard notation and tab for 22 Carter-style solos from bluegrass classics such as: Back Up and Push • The Big Rock Candy Mountain • Cotton Eyed Joe • Cumberland Gap • Down Yonder • Jesse James • John Henry • Little Sadie Long Journey Home • Man of Constant Sorrow • Midnight Special • Mule Skinner Blues • Red Wing • Uncle Joe • The Wabash Cannon Ball • Wildwood Flower • and more.

00699529 .... $8.99

BLUEGRASS GUITAR

Arranged and Performed by Wayne Henderson
Transcribed by David Ziegele

This book/CD pack contains 10 classic bluegrass tunes arranged for solo flatpicking and fingerstyle guitar, in standard notation and tab. The CD features renowned picker Wayne Henderson performing each tune note for note. Includes: Black Mountain Rag • Fisher's Hornpipe • Leather Britches • Lime Rock • Sally Anne • Take Me Out to the Ball Game • Temperence Reel • Twinkle Little Star • and more.

00700184 Book/CD Pack...................... $16.99

BLUEGRASS STANDARDS

by David Hamburger

16 bluegrass classics expertly arranged: Ballad of Jed Clampett • Blue Yodel No. 4 (California Blues) • Can't You Hear Me Calling • I'll Go Stepping Too • I'm Goin' Back to Old Kentucky • Let Me Love You One More Time • My Rose of Old Kentucky • We'll Meet Again Sweetheart • and more.

00699760...$7.99

FRETBOARD ROADMAPS – BLUEGRASS AND FOLK GUITAR

by Fred Sokolow

This book/CD pack will have you playing lead and rhythm anywhere on the fretboard, in any key. You'll learn chord-based licks, moveable major and blues scales, major pentatonic "sliding scales," first-position major scales, and moveable-position major scales. The book includes easy-to-follow diagrams and instructions for beginning, intermediate and advanced players. The CD includes 41 demonstration tracks.

00695355 Book/CD Pack...................... $14.99

THE BIG BOOK OF BLUEGRASS SONGS

The best collection ever of 70+ bluegrass standards! Includes: Alabama Jubilee • Arkansas Traveler • Blue Yodel No. 8 • Cripple Creek • Dark Holler • I Am a Man of Constant Sorrow • I Saw the Light • Orange Blossom Special • Rocky Top • Wayfaring Stranger • Will the Circle Be Unbroken • You Don't Know My Mind • and more.

00311484... $22.99

O BROTHER, WHERE ART THOU?

This songbook features nine selections from the critically-acclaimed Coen brothers film, arranged in melody/lyric/chord format with guitar tab. Songs include: Big Rock Candy Mountain (Harry McClintock) • You Are My Sunshine (Norman Blake) • Hard Time Killing Floor Blues (Chris Thomas King) • I Am a Man of Constant Sorrow (The Soggy Bottom Boys/ Norman Blake) • Keep on the Sunny Side (The Whites) • I'll Fly Away (Alison Krauss and Gillian Welch) • and more.

00313182... $19.99

www.halleonard.com

Prices, contents, and availability subject to change.